How to be People Smart
The Rarest Skill
A Course for Skill with People

Embassy Books
2100 Blossom Way South
St. Petersburg, FL 33712

ISBN 0-9616416-1-4

Library of Congress Catalog N. 77-86285

Foreword

This is not your typical "how to be the best person" book. It's completely different. It's a reminder course, a step-by-step program that gets right to the point of "how to" – How to be People-Smart and how to increase your Skill with People.

Thousands who have used this program will tell you that if you have an open mind and a desire to get more out of life, the concepts outlined in this workbook will work wonders in many ways. It could be the best chance you will ever get to greatly improve the quality of your life.

Capitalize on it!

Les Giblin

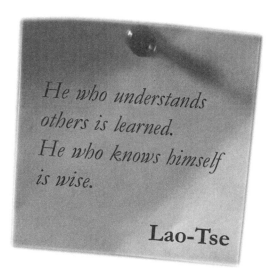

He who understands others is learned. He who knows himself is wise.

Lao-Tse

Table of Contents

> *Education does not mean teaching people what they do not know; it means teaching them to behave as they do not behave.*
>
> **John Ruskin.**

Why So Few People are People Smart

On a People Smart scale of 1-100 it is estimated that the average person would score 10 to 15 and the exceptional 25 to 30. Looking over the knowledge and techniques in this program and seeing how little of it is used can easily verify this.

Why the low scores?

1. Formal education does not include **any** skill with people.

2. To be People Smart – to have skill with people – one has to subordinate one's own human nature. This is a never-ending struggle and there must be frequent reinforcement which few people get.

3. Most individuals who have had some training in effectively dealing with people invariably "self-defeat" when it comes to reinforcing and increasing that knowledge. Almost automatically, those individuals when they see a program like this will react with, "I know all of that" or "I've been through that." Instead they should ask themselves the hard question, "Am I really using this knowledge and technique?" or an even more important question, "Can I get more mileage from this knowledge and technique?"

4. Finally, few people know that KNOWLEDGE DOES NOT HELP YOU - IT IS THE *USE* OF THE KNOWLEDGE THAT BRINGS BENEFITS. It is not what you know; it is how much use you make of what you know that brings the benefits.

Introduction

What, Why, How

What

The primary objective of this program is to *Increase your Skill with People*. You will soon understand the benefits of this, as well as the methods of how to do it.

The program objective - to *Increase your Skill with People* - could be expressed in other ways:

> To make you People Smart
>
> To give you people know-how
>
> To make you more effective with people

No matter what name is put on it, this is an important concept. In fact, it would be very hard to find a more worthy objective. Many authorities will affirm that the greatest help you can get in life – and the greatest kindness you can ever receive – is in this area.

Skill with people also has many other names:

> Leadership
> Salesmanship
> Management ability
> Personality
> Charm

They are all the same!

It has been estimated that 1 in 200 people have true skill with people and are truly People Smart. You are going to be that 1 in 200. All it takes is this course, your open mind and your desire to get more skills and rewards.

Psychologists have proven that the most important factor in your success and well-being is:

> NOT your intelligence
> NOT your education
> NOT physical assets

It is how effective you are with people and increasing your skill with people brings rewards including a:

> Better career
> Better social life
> Better family life

It's because the techniques and rules for more skill with people work on *all* people. The rewards that can come from skill with people are many and varied.

More income	More friends
More recognition	More prestige
More acceptance	More promotion
More approval	More security
More confidence	More satisfaction
More superiority	Less fear
Less worry	

...not to mention success with greater well-being.

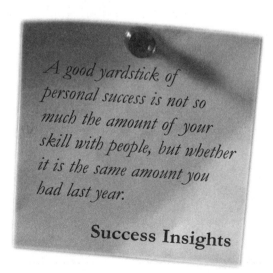

A good yardstick of personal success is not so much the amount of your skill with people, but whether it is the same amount you had last year.

Success Insights

Why

People Smart people are uncommon.

People Smart people are not like most people:

1. Most people do not fully realize the good things that can come from increasing their skill with people. The benefits listed are not just words, they are all very attainable. Anyone can increase skill with people and benefit in many ways.

2. Most people do not realize how easily skill with people can be acquired. All it takes is an understanding of human nature, a new approach and some simple easy-to-do techniques, which this workbook provides.

This book is not about the latest trends in leadership or the current fads in sales. This workbook outlines tried and tested skills developed from years of practice and hard work – the true indicators of success.

People Smart is based on the Lombardi and Rubinstein wisdom that excellence comes from a mastery of the fundamentals – doing the basics well. This program emphasizes the basics, the fundamentals of dealing with people because that is your route to more skill with people and the rewards it brings.

A Closer Look! The immortal football coach Vincent Lombardi, when asked for the secret of his success, answered, "I learned early that excellence comes mostly from a mastery of the fundamentals, doing the basics well. In football the basics are blocking and tackling... My team worked on blocking and tackling over and over, again and again, constantly. In football games the team that does the basics best usually wins. We usually won." The simple philosophy of doing the basics well made him one of the most successful coaches ever and put him in the Football Hall of Fame.

Arthur Rubinstein, world famous pianist, when asked how to become an excellent pianist said, "practice the scales an hour each day like I do." You can best appreciate how profound this statement is by thinking of the intricacy, the complexity and the difficulty of the compositions played by a world-class pianist.

How

In this program the science of learning is fully utilized. How people learn can best be summarized by:

 83% through sight

 11% through hearing

 3% through smell

 2% through touch

 1% through taste

Nearly **95%** of learning takes place through the eyes and ears. This explains why this method of teaching – using pictures, drawings and printed words – combines to give you the maximum impact.

Plus, utilizing another basic rule of learning – we learn by doing – each section ends with an action section to be completed before moving on to the next section. This makes certain of your progress while acknowledging the fact that the *use* of knowledge brings the reward.

The most valuable of all talents is that of never using two words when one will do.

Thomas Jefferson

How to Use This Workbook

Knowledge + Application = Success

Before you can use this proven formula for success you must first reach your moment of truth: You must supply the application.

What you get out of this program depends on you. These skill with people techniques won't help you until you use them. Knowledge itself is of no value. It is the use of knowledge that makes it valuable.

There are three possible outcomes of this program:

✓ Teach you a skill with people you may not know.

✓ Reinforce and remind you of those skills you do know.

✓ Increase your use of this knowledge, so that your benefits are increased.

Simply reading over this program will not be enough. Rather, it takes a step-by-step action plan, making a little improvement each week and adding a little skill on a regular, organized basis.

 Benjamin Franklin tells in an autobiography how he tried for years, with no success, to improve himself and rid himself of certain habits. Then one day he wrote out a list of what he considered to be his shortcomings, such as bad temper, impatience, and lack of consideration for others.

Then he picked what he considered his number one problem. Instead of just making a resolution to improve himself, Franklin made an effort to identify and work on his number one weak spot. One by one, he selected a shortcoming and worked on it. The end result was that within a year he had overcome many bad habits that had been holding him back.

We don't know what your people faults are, but like everyone, you have strengths and weaknesses with people. The point here is that Benjamin Franklin has brilliantly shown us the only effective way to correct faults and weaknesses. We must correct them one at a time, rather than work on all of them at once. Wise old B.F has made your progress toward success and happiness much easier.

As you read through each People Smart skill, we've included "Notes" sections where you can jot down key points or your own ideas. Taking notes and adding your own perspective will allow you to customize this program to your specific needs.

Watch for these icons as you work through this program:

A Closer Look - These are examples of People Smart practices in action. Take a closer look at how others have made these practices work for themselves.

People Smart Best Practices - This calls out and sums up a best practice so you can quickly find it.

Notes - This is where you can write down great ideas and tips, as well as your own plans for putting People Smart practices to work!

Ready-Set-Action - When you see this at the end of each section, it's time to get to work on your own plan of action. Review the key components of a particular practice and write down how you'll put it to work immediately.

People Smart Skill - Use this as your guide to keep track of which skill you're targeting. As you move from skill to skill, the number will change with you.

This step-by-step checklist will keep you on track and help you find your place when you come back for the next skill. After you complete a section, check it off and celebrate! Every step is one step closer to being a People Smart person.

Step-by-step checklist:

Introduction

 People Smart 1

☐ Read pages 15-20

☐ Complete Ready, Set, Action! on page 21

 People Smart 2

☐ Read pages 23-28

☐ Complete Ready, Set, Action! on page 29

 People Smart 3

☐ Read pages 31-34

☐ Complete Ready, Set, Action! on page 35

 People Smart 4

☐ Read pages 37-40

☐ Complete Ready, Set, Action! on page 41

 People Smart 5

☐ Read pages 43-50

☐ Complete Ready, Set, Action! on page 51

 People Smart 6

☐ Read pages 53-56

☐ Complete Ready, Set, Action! on page 57

People Smart 7

☐ Read pages 59-60

☐ Complete Ready, Set, Action!
on page 61

People Smart 9

☐ Read pages 69-72

☐ Complete Ready, Set, Action!
on page 73

People Smart 8

☐ Read pages 63-66

☐ Complete Ready, Set, Action!
on page 67

People Smart 10

☐ Read pages 75-77

☐ Complete Ready, Set, Action!
on page 78

Ladder of self improvement
100 percent – I did it
90 percent – I will
80 percent – I can
70 percent – I think I can
60 percent – I might
50 percent – I think I might
40 percent – what is it?
30 percent – I wish I could
20 percent – I don't know how?
10 percent – I can't
0 percent – I won't

How to Talk to People

People Smart ...Skill! **1**

First things first. Skill with people must start with an understanding of people and human nature. The first thing you must do to be skilled in handling people is to recognize people for what they are!

This may seem simple, but it is a fact that most of us don't do it. We simply are not objective regarding other people.

Whether it is because we do not understand people, really haven't thought about it that much, delude ourselves, or like to rose-color relationships, it creates a road-block to skill with people.

To recognize people for what they are, you have to first acknowledge what people are most interested in:

This is a list of 22 things in which most of us are interested. A good case can be made for many of these to be our #1 interest, keeping in mind our different values and tastes. When you carefully look over this list and think about it, one interest, one thing, stands out far in front. You probably have already selected it; if you haven't, you will agree when it is pointed out:

> *The ability to communicate effectively with others is one of the best talents in life.*
>
> **Millard Bennett**

Love   *Pleasure*   *Money*

Food   *Comfort*   *Clothes*

Status   *Security*   *Education*

Travel   *Leisure*   *Home*

Family   *Relatives*   *Friends*

Themselves   *Peace*   *Freedom*

Religion   *Business*   *Politics*

Sports

People are primarily interested in *themselves*.

Fact: One of the constants of life – it is true now, has always been true and always will be true – is that people want to know what's in it for them, first and foremost.

Fact: Just about all of us are alike in this respect, the exceptions are rare.

Wisdom: We shouldn't be embarrassed or apologetic about this common trait. Man did not make man, God made man and he made him with a nature that is very strong in self-interest .

It is the recognition of this trait that enables us to be People Smart. Let's start with the application of it to skillful conversations – the better words to use, and the better things to talk about.

Notes

_____

_____

_____

_____

_____

_____

_____

_____

*Don't overdo
these four words:*

I, Me, My, Mine

I, me, my, mine

You, Your

*Instead use two
very effective words:*

You, Your

"This is for **you**."…"**You** will benefit."…"**Your** family will,too."… "Doing this will help **you**."

You want to open a safe, but the safe is locked. If you succeed in opening the safe, there will be many good things for you.

You have two sets of numbers. One set will open the safe and you will get your good things. The other set of numbers will not open the safe, but you like them far more than the other numbers.

If you are asked, "Which set of numbers are you going to use to open the safe?" you would reply, "The right numbers, of course."

Now, instead of opening a safe, let's change this to opening up people and instead of sets of numbers, lets change this to sets of words.

Certain words turn people on and certain words turn people off. To attract people to you, you must use the words that turn people on. **You** and **Your** turn people on. **I, me, my** and **mine** turn people off. People will not respond or react favorably to a self-centered **I, me, my** or **mine** approach; they are far more likely to respond favorably to you if you use **you** or **your** to them.

The average person uses a self-centered approach. The People Smart person uses a people-centered approach.

Talk to people about what they are most interested in…themselves.

Just as important as using language centered around the other person, it's also important to talk to people about themselves (**your** work, **your** career, **your** family, **your** welfare, **your** department).

You have a choice.

Choice 1:

You can be the usual conversationalist, expressing your opinions, saying what you think, and talking about what you want to talk about and, in general, being Joe or Jane Average.

Of course, you must keep in mind that Joe and Jane Average are not particularly interesting or exciting to other people.

OR

Choice 2:

You can be the unusual person, the skilled conversationalist, and the person with whom people just love to talk and from whom they welcome conversation.

> **A Closer Look!** For example, you are talking to Mary Brown. You can talk about your successes, the weather, or other people, or you can talk about Mary Brown. When you talk about Mary Brown to Mary Brown, watch her eyes light up, watch her smile, watch her soften, and listen to her tell you that you are so interesting. And, here's the A-ha, you are interesting to Mary Brown. THAT is the point. It is fun to see this happen.

How do you do it? Just select the right subject matter to talk about!

So, how do you get people talking about themselves?

Ask their opinions

> How do you feel about.......?
>
> What do you think of......?
>
> Did you like the results?

Ask them questions about themselves

> Did you enjoy your vacation?
>
> How are things at work?
>
> How are you getting along?

Even better than you talking to people about themselves is getting them talking about themselves! People are much more at ease when they are talking about their favorite subject and will, consequently, respond more favorably to you.

A Closer Look! An insurance agent sold a $500,000 policy to a man who had a dread of doctor offices. The client warned the agent that he would not spend much time in the doctor's office, policy or not. A visit to the doctor for the physical was arranged so that there would be no delay. Unfortunately an emergency patient had to be treated at the last minute and there was a delay. The insurance agent kept the client busy giving his opinions, telling his life story, and answering questions about himself until the emergency patient had been treated.

Simple? Ridiculously simple would be more descriptive. It was also effective and People Smart.

Summary:

Skill with people starts with an understanding of people and human nature. Remember these points about:

Understanding people

1. Recognize people for what they are

2. People are interested in many things, but….

3. People are primarily interested in themselves

Talking to people

1. When talking to people don't overdo **I, me, my** and **mine**

2. Instead use **you** and **your**

3. Talk to people about what they are most interested in: themselves

4. Better yet, get them talking about themselves

A People Smart person asks other people's opinions and gets them talking about themselves.

Notes

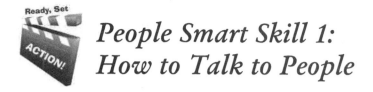

People Smart Skill 1:
How to Talk to People

Attaining Excellence in this Area

Step 1 Analyze yourself on the techniques listed below.

Step 2 Check all the techniques you need to improve.

Step 3 Then for one week, or longer, practice these winning techniques until they are habits.

Concentrate on this one People Smart skill for this week only.

❑ I will remind myself daily that people are primarily interested in themselves.

❑ I will decrease using **I, me, my** and **mine,** and increase my use of **you** and **your.**

❑ I will talk to people about themselves.

❑ I will ask questions about people and ask for their opinions.

❑ I will get people talking about themselves.

Turn the page to complete your
People Smart Journal for the next week.

Week in review

Use this section to create an action plan, celebrate successes and note important insights regarding this People Smart skill.

	Action/Goal	Results	Additional Thoughts
Sunday			
Monday			
Tuesday			
Wednesday			
Thursday			
Friday			
Saturday			

How to Make People Feel Important

People Smart ...Skill! 2

Skill with people comes from the recognition and use of human nature. The key part of this statement is "use of human nature." It is one thing to recognize human nature; it is quite another to put it to work for you. Human nature has often been described as a force not unlike a powerful river or the tides. To harness it, to make it work for you, is truly People Smart.

A Closer Look! *The Hawthorne Experiments*

Conducted between 1924 and 1932 with Western Electric Hawthorn plant employees in Cicero, Illinois, in which a group of plant workers on a sub-assembly job were observed to measure how adjusting the environment impacted productivity.

When the company added an incentive, production rose. They added a second incentive and production increased again. They added a third incentive and production increased again.

Some of the engineers decided to see what would happen when incentives were removed. When they took away the first incentive, production increased again. They took away the second and third incentives and the same thing happened. In an effort to reverse the trend, the engineers adjusted the workspace: raising benches, lowering chairs and introducing poor lighting. Production again increased to the highest point ever reached.

The final analysis? This is an outstanding example of the principle of making people feel important and the significance of social dynamics. The workers were the focus of years of studies and observations, they were kept informed, and they were given a chance to be heard. They wanted to please the researchers whose attention was making them feel good.

The more important you make people feel, the more they will like you and respond to you.

What makes us tick?

Our strongest trait is self-preservation; the desire to live takes center stage when we are in danger or peril. It isn't often – maybe only a few times in our lives – that we are in danger or think we are in danger. When that happens, our instinct for survival immediately takes over, automatically, without thinking. Nothing else matters – not money, not property, not appearances. We just want to get out in one piece.

It's not everyday that our strongest trait is called into use. As such, it means that our everyday traits take on added importance. Yet, very few of us recognize what is our next strongest trait: the desire to be important.

The desire to be important makes people tick; when you know this you have an insight into people.

Everyone wants to be treated as a somebody. Making people feel important turns them on. If you let people be the "big dog" they will like you. Making yourself important turns people off; if you make yourself the "big dog," thereby making them the "little dog," they will resent you.

When you make people feel important, you are increasing their self-esteem. Self-esteem is extremely important to all of us because we all want to feel good about ourselves, and it is much easier to do it when other people treat us well.

Is it any wonder that people respond to those who make them feel good? Actually, the ability to make people feel important is the keystone of personal charm. How simple it is when you analyze it!

How do you make people feel important?

1. Skillfully listen to them

Listening to people is the best way to make them feel important. When you listen to people you are letting them know that they are important enough that you will listen. You are letting them know that you respect them and their opinion matters.

Of course, this flatters the other person and it increases their self-esteem. It increases their opinion of you; consequently, they respond to you. Usually, the mere fact that you are listening is enough to endear you to them. Conversely, failure to listen to people is the surest way to make people feel unimportant and make them feel like nobodies. **(Remember, everybody wants to feel like a somebody.)**

2. Applaud and compliment people

When they deserve it…people love to be appreciated, applauded and complimented. Sociologists say it is a basic drive in all of us and that it is only natural for people to respond to those who applaud and compliment them. Not only is the response a natural reaction, but something else makes it even more powerful:

There is a rarity of applause and compliments in our everyday lives, not because we don't deserve a bit of applause now and then and an occasional compliment, but because nobody dishes them out.

Most of us are so *I*-oriented that we really don't think very much about the other person. Observation and listening will verify the rareness of applause and compliments.

Experts who want something will first pay a sincere compliment and then make their request. It works every time! That is really People Smart.

3. Use people's names as often as possible.

Connect with others by using the other person's name 10 times in the first minute of conversation:

> "Hi **Sam**, how are you today?"

> "**Sam,** it is good seeing you."

> "Please sit down, **Sam**."

> "**Sam,** you are looking good."

> "**Sam,** how's the family?"

You get the picture. All exaggeration aside, we all have a wish: We want to be treated as individuals, not as part of a group. What makes us individuals is the most individual thing we own – our name.

Note the differences when using a name or not using a name.

Good morning.	Good morning, Helen.
Thank you.	Thank you, Mr. Gomez.
It was a pleasure.	It was a pleasure, Jim.

Hearing and seeing their names gives people a feeling of importance, a sense of belonging. That is the reason for nameplates on desks and name badges on people.

 Attach names to your sentences and include names frequently in your conversation.

4. Pause slightly before answering people.

When someone asks you a question or waits for your comments, pause for a few seconds before you say what you are going to say. This is excellent psychology and a subtlety of the highest rank. When you pause before answering, you increase the other person's self-esteem. You give the impression that their question was intelligent, you flatter them by giving the courtesy of considering what they said.

Conversely, when you fire back an answer immediately, you do the exact opposite. You create the impression that you didn't even think over their words, causing them to feel brushed off or belittled. This doesn't always happen, but the risk is there and it is so unnecessary.

 Pausing a few seconds and then voicing your thoughts is a People Smart technique that makes the speaker feel listened to and respected.

5. Acknowledge people who are waiting to see or hear from you.

Simply let other people know that you know they are waiting. Return phone calls and correspondence promptly and provide interim phone calls and explanatory letters or emails when you don't have a final disposition. When you acknowledge people, you are treating them as somebodies. People are always easier to deal with when they are acknowledged.

6. Talk to them about them; use you and your to give people a feeling of importance.

When you use **you** and **your**, you are making the other person the important one. When you use **I, me, my** and **mine**, you are making yourself the important one.

Notes

Summary:

The strongest trait in human beings is the desire for self-preservation.
The next strongest trait is the desire to be important. The more important you make people feel, the more they will like you and respond to you.

You make people feel important by believing that they ARE important and then.....

- ✓ Skillfully listen to them
- ✓ Applaud and compliment them
- ✓ Use their names often
- ✓ Pause before answering them
- ✓ Acknowledge people waiting to see or hear from you
- ✓ In talking to them, use *you* and *your* instead of *I*, *me*, *my* and *mine*

One touch of nature makes the whole world kin.

William Shakespeare

People Smart Skill 2:
How to Make People Feel Important

Attaining Excellence in this Area

Step 1   Analyze yourself on the techniques listed below.

Step 2   Check all the techniques you need to improve.

Step 3   Then for one week, or longer, practice these winning techniques until they are habits.

Concentrate on this one People Smart skill for this week only.

❑ I will skillfully listen to people.

❑ I will applaud and compliment people.

❑ I will use their names often.

❑ I will pause before answering them.

❑ I will acknowledge people who are waiting to see or hear from me.

❑ I will use *you* and *your* in talking to people.

Turn the page to complete your
People Smart Journal for the next week.

Week in review

Use this section to create an action plan, celebrate successes and note important insights regarding this People Smart skill.

	Action/Goal	Results	Additional Thoughts
Sunday	------------------- ------------------- -------------------	------------------- ------------------- -------------------	-------------------------------- -------------------------------- --------------------------------
Monday	------------------- ------------------- -------------------	------------------- ------------------- -------------------	-------------------------------- -------------------------------- --------------------------------
Tuesday	------------------- ------------------- -------------------	------------------- ------------------- -------------------	-------------------------------- -------------------------------- --------------------------------
Wednesday	------------------- ------------------- -------------------	------------------- ------------------- -------------------	-------------------------------- -------------------------------- --------------------------------
Thursday	------------------- ------------------- -------------------	------------------- ------------------- -------------------	-------------------------------- -------------------------------- --------------------------------
Friday	------------------- ------------------- -------------------	------------------- ------------------- -------------------	-------------------------------- -------------------------------- --------------------------------
Saturday	------------------- ------------------- -------------------	------------------- ------------------- -------------------	-------------------------------- -------------------------------- --------------------------------

How to Agree with People  3

Of all the good techniques for skill with people, there is one that is unsurpassed and remarkably simple!

Master the art of being agreeable.

1. Be agreeable...agree with people.

Develop an agreeable nature. As a wise man once said, "Any fool can *disagree* with people; it takes a smart man, a shrewd man, to *agree* with people."

A popular customer service slogan states that "the customer is always right." Agree, even when the other person is wrong. When you agree with people you make them feel good and you enhance their self-opinion, which is everybody's want and need. In return, they will like you and respond to you. It's a simple trade: you agree with them; they respond to you.

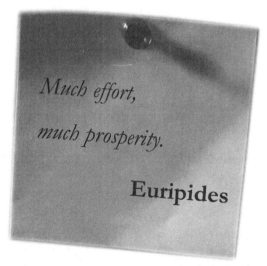

Much effort, much prosperity.

Euripides

 The art of being agreeable is an essential People Smart asset.

2. The art of being agreeable is more than being agreeable. It includes communicating that fact to other people. You do this by nodding your head and saying the magic words, "You are right" and "I agree with you." These magic words resonate with people. Consider the opposite approach: shaking your head no and disagreeing with the speaker. Is it any wonder this behavior meets with resistance?

3. Admit it when you are wrong: When you are wrong, say it out loud: "I was wrong", or "I made a mistake". It takes a big person to admit an error and doing so gains the respect and admiration of others. In the end, that is what matters most.

 Let's revisit our little dog/big dog again. Our little dog doesn't quite know about people as much as our big dog, who has quite the strong character. When the little dog is a bad dog, he will invariably do one of three things: lie (I couldn't help it), alibi (I didn't do it), or deny (It wasn't my fault).

People being people, or dogs being dogs in this case, there is no way the little dog can win with such tactics. People will look down on the little dog and invariably he will lose more than he would have by simply admitting to being wrong.

On the other hand, the big dog, because of his skill with people and stronger character, admits to being wrong when he is wrong and winds up being the leader of the pack.

We all admire people who have the strength and character to say "I was wrong" or "I made a mistake."

4. Don't disagree (out loud) unless it is absolutely necessary. Of course, there are many times when it is not possible or practical to agree. Nonetheless, most disagreements are completely unnecessary and, actually, they are more a clash of egos and conflicting ideas. Mind, you are not expected to be a hypocrite or compromise your self-respect, principles, pride, integrity or personal policy. You should speak out – clearly and distinctly – if these are called into question. The point is that most disagreements are unnecessary and the art of being agreeable is an excellent People Smart Asset.

You will gain much more by not disagreeing with people than you will by disagreeing with them. Before disagreeing, People Smart people ask whether the disagreement is really necessary.

There are three reasons for the art of being agreeable:

1. People like those who agree with them.

2. People dislike those who disagree with them.

3. People dislike being disagreed with.

The best People Smart techniques do not work all of the time.

It is not said here that they do or that it is intended that they should. What is the case is that People Smart techniques work most of the time and, more importantly, work better than alternative ways. Sometimes, with the art of being agreeable, there are times when you should speak out, when you must speak out, and when it would be folly and impractical to agree with the other person. However, those times are few and far between. Objective analysis will show almost all disagreements to be unnecessary; they could and should be avoided.

The ends of life are not Knowledge, but Action.

Thomas Huxley

Summary

Skill with People includes mastering the art of being agreeable. This technique is very simple:

1. Be agreeable, agree with people.

2. Tell people when you agree with them.

3. If you can't agree, and often you can't, just don't disagree, unless it is absolutely necessary.

4. When you are wrong, admit it.

Notes

People Smart Skill 3:
How to Agree with People

Attaining Excellence in this Area

Step 1   Analyze yourself on the techniques listed below.

Step 2   Check all the techniques you need to improve.

Step 3   Then for one week, or longer, practice these winning techniques until they are habits.

Concentrate on this one People Smart skill for this week only.

❑   I will be naturally agreeable.

❑   I will tell people when I agree with them by using phrases such as, "I agree with you" and "You are right."

❑   I will not disagree out loud unless it is absolutely necessary.

❑   I will admit when I am wrong.

Turn the page to complete your
People Smart Journal for the next week.

Week in review

Use this section to create an action plan, celebrate successes and note important insights regarding this People Smart skill.

	Action/Goal	Results	Additional Thoughts
Sunday	------------------- ------------------- -------------------	------------------- ------------------- -------------------	------------------------------- ------------------------------- -------------------------------
Monday	------------------- ------------------- -------------------	------------------- ------------------- -------------------	------------------------------- ------------------------------- -------------------------------
Tuesday	------------------- -------------------	------------------- -------------------	------------------------------- -------------------------------
Wednesday	------------------- ------------------- -------------------	------------------- ------------------- -------------------	------------------------------- ------------------------------- -------------------------------
Thursday	------------------- ------------------- -------------------	------------------- ------------------- -------------------	------------------------------- ------------------------------- -------------------------------
Friday	------------------- ------------------- -------------------	------------------- ------------------- -------------------	------------------------------- ------------------------------- -------------------------------
Saturday	------------------- ------------------- -------------------	------------------- ------------------- -------------------	------------------------------- ------------------------------- -------------------------------

How to Be People Smart

How to Listen to People  4

Good listening skills are doubly important, for the ability to listen well is the number one social asset, as well as being a career must!

Listening skill is also a tremendous personal asset. You are more effective with people when you are listening, than when you are talking.

✓ The more listening you do, the better you will be liked.

✓ The more listening you do, the smarter you will become. You learn more by listening than you do by talking. You add what the other person knows to what you know. Two "knows are better than one." When asked why he rarely spoke, the late Sid Richardson, who left an estate of several hundred million dollars, said it best: "I ain't learning when I'm talking."

Listening, not imitation, may be the sincerest form of flattery.

Joyce Brothers

✓ The more listening you do, the better conversationalist you will be. When you listen to people you are allowing them to hear their favorite speaker. Listening is a much bigger part of being a good conversationalist; you are increasing their self-esteem, and you are earning their gratitude.

Clearly, the advantages of being a good listener are tremendous.

The five rules for being a skillful listener are:

1. Look at the person who is speaking and keep looking as long as that person is talking. Being a skillful listener is no accident. You should listen with your eyes as well as your ears. Anybody worth listening to is worth looking at. When you listen with your ears and eyes, several things happen:

✓ You pay people a compliment.

✓ You show them you are listening

✓ You get a complete picture of what they're saying because you see the non-verbals of their communication, as well as their verbals.

 Looking at people when they are talking to you is very People Smart.

2. Listen intently and lean toward the speaker. Give the impression you are intensely interested; appear as if you don't want to miss a single word. The expression on your face is the barometer of your interest. Leaning toward the speaker is excellent psychology.

 Leaning toward the person who is speaking is very People Smart.

3. Ask questions. There are two reasons you should ask questions: Questions let the speaker know that you are listening and questions are a subtle form of flattery. Questions are preferable to comments in the science of listening. The questions can be as simple as:

✓ Then what happened?

✓ How long did it take?

✓ How did you come out?

✓ Would you do it again?

Asking questions lets the speaker know you're engaged and makes the speaker feel good.

4. Don't interrupt and don't change topics. Interrupting is the most common fault in listening. A major step in increasing listening skills is the elimination of all interruptions of other people and things in your conversations. Interrupting is not always intentional and is done sometimes by those unaware they're doing it. The abrupt change to a new subject or a switch of subjects is the same as interrupting. People greatly resent being interrupted and resent those who do it. Interrupting and changing topics are nothing more than discourtesy and bad manners.

As a People Smart expert, you know that interrupting and abruptly changing the topic are both a loser and a no-no. The answer is more patience and more self-discipline.

5. When commenting or joining into conversation, use **you** and **your**, not **I, me, my** or **mine**. When you use **you**, you keep the focus on the speaker. When you use **I**, you switch focus to yourself. You've changed the entire relationship! Remember earlier in "How to Talk to People" the importance of using the right words was explained. Specifically, when you use **you** or **your** to people you turn them on, and when you use **I, me, my** or **mine** you turn people off.

Focusing on the other person by using you *and* your *in your conversations shows common sense, is effective and People Smart.*

Summary:

Listening skills is a tremendous personal asset. The better you listen:

- ✓ The better you will be liked.
- ✓ The smarter you will become.
- ✓ The better conversationalist you will be.

The five rules for skillful listening are:

1. Look at the person who is talking and keep looking as long as that person is talking.

2. Listen intently and lean toward the speaker.

3. Ask questions.

4. Don't interrupt and don't change topics.

5. In commenting or joining in the talk, use **you** and **your** not **I, me, my** or **mine**.

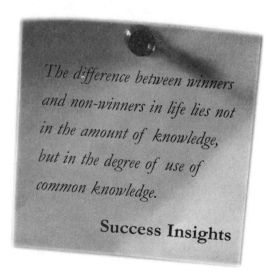

The difference between winners and non-winners in life lies not in the amount of knowledge, but in the degree of use of common knowledge.

Success Insights

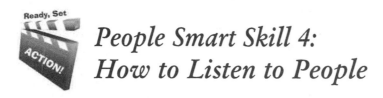

People Smart Skill 4:
How to Listen to People

Attaining Excellence in this Area

Step 1   Analyze yourself on the techniques listed below.

Step 2   Check all the techniques you need to improve.

Step 3   Then for one week, or longer, practice these winning techniques until they are habits.

Concentrate on this one People Smart skill for this week only.

❑   I will look at people when they are talking.

❑   I will listen intently and lean toward the speaker.

❑   I will ask questions.

❑   I won't interrupt or change topics.

❑   I will comment using *you* or *your*.

Turn the page to complete your
People Smart Journal for the next week.

Week in review

Use this section to create an action plan, celebrate successes and note important insights regarding this People Smart skill.

	Action/Goal	Results	Additional Thoughts
Sunday	------------------- ------------------- -------------------	------------------- ------------------- -------------------	------------------------------- ------------------------------- -------------------------------
Monday	------------------- ------------------- -------------------	------------------- ------------------- -------------------	------------------------------- ------------------------------- -------------------------------
Tuesday	------------------- ------------------- -------------------	------------------- ------------------- -------------------	------------------------------- ------------------------------- -------------------------------
Wednesday	------------------- ------------------- -------------------	------------------- ------------------- -------------------	------------------------------- ------------------------------- -------------------------------
Thursday	------------------- ------------------- -------------------	------------------- ------------------- -------------------	------------------------------- ------------------------------- -------------------------------
Friday	------------------- ------------------- -------------------	------------------- ------------------- -------------------	------------------------------- ------------------------------- -------------------------------
Saturday	------------------- ------------------- -------------------	------------------- ------------------- -------------------	------------------------------- ------------------------------- -------------------------------

How to Be People Smart

How to Influence People

People Smart

5

...Skill!

Influence – how to get people to do what you want them to do – involves the use of simple logic applied to human nature. There is one big secret in successfully influencing others; when you know this secret, you can easily become skilled in this field. To open people up, to move them, first find out what they want.

> **A Closer Look!** The typical diner struggles with the task of opening clams and oysters. Without know-how, opening them is a big task. Too little pressure will not open them; pressure in the wrong spots will not open them; too much pressure, as with a hammer, will ruin them; yet experts open them almost as fast as the eyes can see.
>
> As it is with clams and oysters, so it is with influencing people – just knowing how to go about it, having the know-how and using it properly simplifies the task and the results are far more rewarding.

When you know **what** will move them, you then know **how** to move them.

Which button for which person?

Prestige?	*Recognition?*	*Security?*
Satisfaction?	*Superiority?*	*Ego?*
Money?	*Friendship?*	*Do good?*

Look around you. Think about all the people you know and the first thing you will notice is that people are different in many ways. They dress differently, eat differently, live differently, go to different churches, and have different lifestyles and tastes. So in order to influence them, we must first find out what moves them. Different things move different people. People do and do not do things for many reasons.

Wisdom comes from matching people to their tastes and desires. When we know what people want we then know how to move them. The problem here is that we have a strong tendency to assume that what we want and like is what other people will want and like. It doesn't work that way! People have their own values, their own desires, and their own tastes.

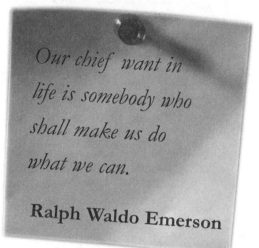

Our chief want in life is somebody who shall make us do what we can.

Ralph Waldo Emerson

Find out what they want, what they are after and then...

Show people how they can get what they want, by doing what you want them to do.

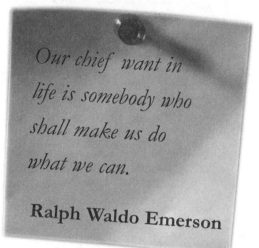

A Closer Look! Let's take a look at successful politicians. They want people to vote for them and get them to do it by promising or giving the impression it is to the voters' interest to do so. Specifically, when the politicians talk to labor, they talk labor, when they talk to business, they talk business, when they talk to senior citizens, they talk about their interests, and when they talk to farmers, they talk about their interests. In other words, the politicians fit their appeal to audiences.

It should be no different with us in our daily lives. When we want people to do something we should fit our appeal to their interests.

Push the hot buttons

Tell people what they want to hear; use their desires to move them. You will be utterly amazed at how easy it is to get people to do what you want them to do when you show an interest in their interests, speak their language, and make a connection with them.

The person   *The hot button*

Vain person . . . . .Build his/her ego.

Philanthropist . . . . .Discuss charity and the well-being of others.

Proud person . . . . .Talk about accomplishments.

Team player . . . . .Focus on the benefits for the group.

Family person . . . . .Demonstrate the benefits for his/her family.

Money-conscious person . . . . . . .Show cost savings and efficiencies.

Someone desiring security . . . . . .Discuss quality, longevity and security.

Recognition-hungry person . . . . .How will recognition be granted?

Notes
_____
_____
_____
_____
_____
_____

The skill to influence people is to push the right buttons.

How do you know what people want?

It is not difficult to determine other people's values, what they want, what they like.

Ask them questions:

What do you want most from your work?
What do you want most from life?
What do you value the most?

Listen to their responses. This is your way of knowing them.

Watch people. They tell you many things by their actions, often more so than by their words.

A Closer Look! If a famous author and speaker were asked if one of his books was any good, he wouldn't reply, "I think it's a great book." Instead, he would use the third-person technique, saying, "Over 300,000 people bought it." Likewise, if someone asked him if his seminar was worthwhile, he would reply, "Three hundred companies repeated it."

Notes _____

_____

_____

_____

_____

_____

Finally, *study* people. They are fascinating and interesting subject matter, one with which you will never get bored.

You will note a common denominator in these four ways of finding out about people: You have to be people minded. Most of us are too self-oriented, we don't ask, we don't listen well, we aren't observant; we don't study people. This is primarily because we don't care that much or we aren't interested. The result is that we miss a lot of benefits that come from skill with people.

To convince people, speak through "third persons."

You can be more convincing and more persuasive if you go at it in the right way. When you are trying to make a point, don't say it yourself, make your point by the third-person technique. Note the difference between: 'I believe,' 'I say,' or 'I feel' and 'Bill Jones says,' 'I saw in the paper that,' or 'I heard on the radio that....'

Why?   Even though they may not believe you, people will believe third persons.

The third-person technique can be used the following three ways:

" " Quotes: "The Smith Co. says it is the best on the market."
"Bill Jones says this new material is the answer."
"Mrs. Anderson, just widowed, says thank heavens for the insurance!"

$ Bring in success stories: The Jones Co. sold over $8000 worth the first week.
Your neighbor made $X on it.

fact Use facts and figures: Over 100,000 people use this.
We do business with 100 of your friends and neighbors.

It is human nature for people to be skeptical when you say something in your own favor; when others say it people will be more likely to accept it. It is a simple matter of your own credibility.

Using the third-person technique – a built-in testimonial – to convince people is People Smart.

Using the third-person technique greatly increases your credibility! You are more believable, more convincing, more persuasive, and you can even make your statements stronger.

If you are selling your car for $10,000 and the prospective buyer questions the selling price, what carries more weight?

I believe $10,000 is a very fair price.

The auto blue book has $11,000 for this car...or the used car lots are getting $10,800 for models not as good as this one.

If you are selling your house and want $200,000 for it, but the potential buyer only wants to offer $170,000, what carries more weight?

> I carefully researched other houses like this and the price is competitive.

> The house was appraised two weeks ago for just over this price.

The second answer in each example is the better one, of course!

Let the third-person technique be your defense. Quote, cite, bring in supporting facts.

New faces...have more authority than accustomed ones.

Euripides

Summary:

Influencing others begins with recognizing what matters most to them, not you.

1. There is one big secret in successful influence.

2. Before you can influence people, you must find out what moves them.

3. Then show them how they can get what they want by doing what you want them to do.

4. To find out what people want, ask them, listen to them and study them.

5. To convince people, speak through the third-person technique.

6. You can do away with skepticism, you can make your statements stronger, and you can convince people faster by quoting others instead of saying it yourself.

Notes

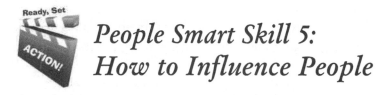

People Smart Skill 5:
How to Influence People

Attaining Excellence in this Area

Step 1   Analyze yourself on the techniques listed below.

Step 2   Check all the techniques you need to improve.

Step 3   Then for one week, or longer, practice these winning techniques until they are habits.

Concentrate on this one People Smart skill for this week only.

❑   I will influence people by finding out what they want, their likes, their values, and their needs.

❑   I will do this by listening to them, by asking them and by studying them.

❑   I will then show them how they can get what they want by doing what I want them to do.

❑   I will convince them by using the third-person technique.

Turn the page to complete your
People Smart Journal for the next week.

Week in review

Use this section to create an action plan, celebrate successes and note important insights regarding this People Smart skill.

	Action/Goal	Results	Additional Thoughts
Sunday	-------------------	-------------------	-----------------------------------
	-------------------	-------------------	-----------------------------------
	-------------------	-------------------	-----------------------------------
Monday	-------------------	-------------------	-----------------------------------
	-------------------	-------------------	-----------------------------------
	-------------------	-------------------	-----------------------------------
Tuesday	-------------------	-------------------	-----------------------------------
	-------------------	-------------------	-----------------------------------
	-------------------	-------------------	-----------------------------------
Wednesday	-------------------	-------------------	-----------------------------------
	-------------------	-------------------	-----------------------------------
	-------------------	-------------------	-----------------------------------
Thursday	-------------------	-------------------	-----------------------------------
	-------------------	-------------------	-----------------------------------
	-------------------	-------------------	-----------------------------------
Friday	-------------------	-------------------	-----------------------------------
	-------------------	-------------------	-----------------------------------
	-------------------	-------------------	-----------------------------------
Saturday	-------------------	-------------------	-----------------------------------
	-------------------	-------------------	-----------------------------------
	-------------------	-------------------	-----------------------------------

How to Make up People's Minds  6

Skill with people should include the ability to make up their minds for them. To get favorable decisions from people, don't depend on luck or guesswork or whims. Those skilled in human relations have technique, which greatly increase their chances of getting people to say yes. Getting people to say yes simply means getting them to make up their minds favorably.

The phrase skill with people (People Smart) has been used many times in this workbook. Getting people to say yes to you, getting them to act favorably toward you, is the ultimate in People Smart. Here are some techniques that will greatly increase your power with people which are also fun to use.

1. Give people reasons to say YES to you.

Most everything is done for a reason, so when you want people to do something, give them a reason to do it. When you give people reasons, they will be far more likely to do what you want them to do. But make sure the reasons you give them are their reasons, not your reasons. Using **their** reasons mean showing them **their** advantages and **their** benefits.

Your Reasons **VS.** *You'll save money. It will help you. You'll meet new people.*

The best time to give people their reasons for saying yes to you is when they are making up their minds. Timing is important in most everything. In getting favorable decisions from people, time is crucial. Giving people their reasons exactly when they are making up their minds is usually the deciding factor. If you have already given them their reasons and they still are hesitating or debating, repeat the reasons or give new ones.

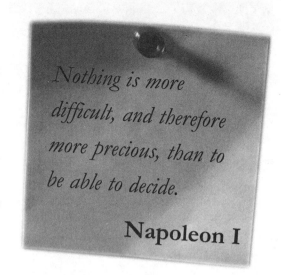

Nothing is more difficult, and therefore more precious, than to be able to decide.

Napoleon I

2. Ask YES questions.

Yes questions are questions that can only be answered with yes. Think about how you would answer these questions:

> Q: You want your family to be happy, don't you?
> A: YES!
>
> Q: You like to enjoy yourself, don't you?
> A: YES!

The idea of YES questions is simple: You multiply your chances of getting a yes when you get people into "yes frame of mind."

When people have said yes to you several times it is much easier for them – and far more probable – to say yes to your proposal, idea or request. Not only are YES questions effective, they are fun to use and fun to see work.

There are two other important techniques to use when asking YES questions – be sure to nod your head while asking the questions and begin the questions with a *you* orientation.

> *Would you like to earn more money?*
>
> *Would you like to have a job where you have fun?*
>
> *Is flexibility important to you?*

3. Give people a choice between two YES answers.

Use loaded questions: Give people a choice between saying yes to you one way or saying yes to you another way, by loading the question.

To get a person to work overtime: Will you work tonight or do you prefer to work tomorrow night?

To get an appointment: May I see you in the morning or do you prefer the afternoon?

Either way the answer is a YES.

When you give people a choice between saying yes and yes, you're giving them a choice between doing what you want them to do one way or doing what you want them to do another way.

In the example above, the poorer way to ask the question would be, "Will you work overtime and may I see you tomorrow? The loaded question gets a yes and the poorly worded question may likely get a no!

 Giving people a choice between two YES answers is People Smart.

4. Let people know you expect them to say YES.

People being people, human nature being what it is, when you want people to do something, one of the better ways for you to get them to do it is to let them know they are expected to say yes. You will be surprised at the number of people who need no other reason to do things than they are expected to do them.

Of course you will want to earn this incentive.

All team members are expected to attend meetings.

Show strength, show firmness, be definite and you will be astonished at the YES answers you get from people.

This technique doesn't work all the time but it works most of the time and it works better than alternative methods. Try it. See for yourself!

These four techniques for making up people's minds are prime examples of people know-how. It is the *use* of know-how that creates skilled people. Remember, you should not depend on luck, guesswork or another person's whims. The reasons, of course, you now know. There is no need to do so. There are better ways as these four techniques prove.

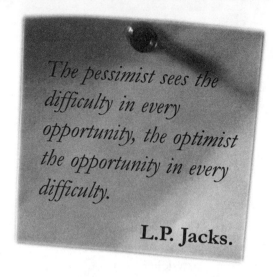

The pessimist sees the difficulty in every opportunity, the optimist the opportunity in every difficulty.

L.P. Jacks.

Actually these four techniques are the techniques used by top salesmen to close sales. They use them to get their customers to act, to buy, to say yes, and that is exactly the same as wanting people to say yes to you.

Use these four simple techniques and remember it is the use of knowledge that makes People Smart.

Summary:

To get favorable decisions from people, don't depend on luck, guesswork or their whims. There are four techniques for getting people to say YES:

1. Give people reasons to say YES to you.

2. Ask yes questions and get people into a "YES frame of mind." Nod YES while asking the question and begin them with a **you** orientation.

3. Give people a choice between two YES answers.

4. Let people know that they are expected to say YES to you.

Power and skill with people comes from the use of know-how. These are prime examples of know-how that will increase your power and skill with people.

People Smart Skill 6:
How to Make up People's Minds

Attaining Excellence in this Area

Step 1   Analyze yourself on the techniques listed below.

Step 2   Check all the techniques you need to improve.

Step 3   Then for one week, or longer, practice these winning techniques until they are habits.

Concentrate on this one People Smart skill for this week only.

❏   I will give people their reasons to say YES to me.

❏   I will get them into a "YES frame of mind" by asking YES questions, nodding my head yes and starting the questions with a **you** orientation.

❏   I will give people a choice between two YES answers.

❏   I will let people know they are expected to say YES to me.

Turn the page to complete your
People Smart Journal for the next week.

Week in review

Use this section to create an action plan, celebrate successes and note important insights regarding this People Smart skill.

	Action/Goal	Results	Additional Thoughts
Sunday	------------------- ------------------- -------------------	------------------- ------------------- -------------------	----------------------------- ----------------------------- -----------------------------
Monday	------------------- ------------------- -------------------	------------------- ------------------- -------------------	----------------------------- ----------------------------- -----------------------------
Tuesday	------------------- ------------------- -------------------	------------------- ------------------- -------------------	----------------------------- ----------------------------- -----------------------------
Wednesday	------------------- ------------------- -------------------	------------------- ------------------- -------------------	----------------------------- ----------------------------- -----------------------------
Thursday	------------------- ------------------- -------------------	------------------- ------------------- -------------------	----------------------------- ----------------------------- -----------------------------
Friday	------------------- ------------------- -------------------	------------------- ------------------- -------------------	----------------------------- ----------------------------- -----------------------------
Saturday	------------------- ------------------- -------------------	------------------- ------------------- -------------------	----------------------------- ----------------------------- -----------------------------

How to Set People's Moods  **7**

The first few seconds of any relationship usually sets the tone and spirit of it. The 2nd basic law of human behavior is: *People strongly tend to respond in kind to the behavior of other people.*

When you have the ability to put people into a good or friendly mood, you greatly increase your chances of getting them to do what you want them to do. Skillfully setting peoples moods is not that difficult when you go at it in the right way.

Plus, timing is everything! It is at the start of your dealings with people that you can best set their moods, because the tone and the spirit at the start is usually the tone and spirit of the entire relationship.

It costs so little. I wonder why we give little thought to a smile, kind words, a glance, a touch. What magic by them is wrought?

Carolyn Ruth Howel

Here is people know-how at its best. You can make 9 out of 10 people friendly, courteous, and cooperative in one second. How? In the first second – that instant when you establish eye contact before you say anything – give people your sincere smile. They will respond in kind.

This is the surest, fastest, easiest way for you to win people over. This simple technique is a must with experts and should be a must for you. If you don't use this technique, it will take much work and time (hours, days or even weeks) on your part to get people into the same warm, friendly mood you could have gotten *in one second*. Remember to smile before you break the silence, before you say the first hello, before you say anything. A smile before you say anything is much more effective than at any other time.

 If you put out a blizzard, back will come a blizzard; if you put out sunshine, back will come sunshine. People Smart people use this technique to warm up people.

Summary:
The first few seconds of meeting someone usually sets the tone and spirit of the entire relationship.

1. Remember the second basic law of human behavior: people strongly tend to respond in kind to the behavior of other people. With this law, you can make 9 out of 10 people friendly, courteous, and co-operative in one second.

2. In the first second when you first establish eye contact, before you say anything, give people your sincere smile.

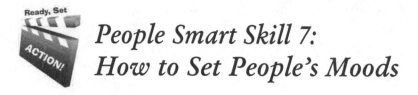

People Smart Skill 7:
How to Set People's Moods

Attaining Excellence in this Area

Step 1   Analyze yourself on the techniques listed below.

Step 2   Check all the techniques you need to improve.

Step 3   Then for one week, or longer, practice these winning techniques until they are habits.

Concentrate on this one People Smart skill for this week only.

❑   I will sincerely smile before I say anything to anybody.

❑   I will remember the 2nd basic law of human behavior: People respond in kind.

❑   I will remember that with people, sunshine begets sunshine and blizzards beget blizzards.

❑   I will make a concerted effort to be friendlier and more pleasant.

Turn the page to complete your
People Smart Journal for the next week.

Week in review

Use this section to create an action plan, celebrate successes and note important insights regarding this People Smart skill.

	Action/Goal	Results	Additional Thoughts
Sunday			
Monday			
Tuesday			
Wednesday			
Thursday			
Friday			
Saturday			

How to Praise People

Man does not live on bread alone. As a matter of fact, he needs food for the spirit as well as for the body. Remember how you feel when a kind word or compliment is given to you? Remember how long the good feeling lasts? Sometimes it lasts for several days.

What can be the big profit in your own experiences of this kind? Is it that others will react just as you do?

Be generous with praise. It's not about how you feel giving the praise, or that you walked on clouds as a result of doing it, or even that the good feeling lasted for awhile. The lesson in giving praise is if you react that way, so will other people!

Praise is the food of the spirit, praise turns people on, praise will endear you to people, praise will give you people power, making you People Smart.

 If you want to be better liked, have more friends, be a better person, and be truly People Smart, look for something and somebody to praise and then do it.

Like so many things, there is fine print.

Say the kind of things to people so that they, and you, will be glad you spoke.

Praise should never be about regrets, regretful remarks, or second-guessing.

Make your praise sincere.

Experts have long taught that sincerity is an absolute must in proper praise. If your praise is not sincere, do not give it. Insincere praise is much worse than no praise. Insincere praise has been described as a million dollar insult to another. All of us know people who are generous with praise and yet are disliked or resented because their praise is not sincere. Used properly, praise is a tremendous tool. Used improperly, it is a boomerang.

Praise the act not the person.

When you praise people, you:

✓ Often embarrass them

✓ Often confuse them

✓ Lay yourself open to charges of favoritism

When you praise acts, you avoid all this plus create an incentive for more.

> **Wrong:** **Ms. Smith, you did a great job!**
>
> **Better:** **Ms. Smith, your work on the Jones account, particularly regarding the savings you are finding by using your cost accounting approach, is superb.**
>
> **Wrong:** **Mr. Jones, you are a great guy.**
>
> **Better:** **Mr. Jones, your overtime work has been a great help and we appreciate your attitude.**

Here is a happiness formula that is good business also: Say daily one kind thing to at least three people. Get into this excellent habit. It will bring you more return for less output than almost anything you can do.

This is a happiness formula for you as you are the prime beneficiary from this pleasant skill with people. When you see the appreciation and joy on the faces of those to whom you have said kind things, then you will enjoy more of life and yourself. Enjoying yourself is one of the major victories of life.

You also help other people by increasing their self-esteem and making them feel good about themselves.

A multiplicity of good comes from this simple People Smart technique.

The sooner you start, the sooner the benefits.

Notes

Summary:

As in People Smart 7, it's important to remember that the first few seconds usually sets the tone and spirit of the entire relationship.

1. Remember that man does not live on bread alone, that he needs food for the spirit as well as for the body.

2. Be generous with praise.

3. However, the praise must be sincere

4. Praise the act, not the person.

5. Use the happiness formula: say daily one kind thing to at least 3 people and see how you feel.

Notes

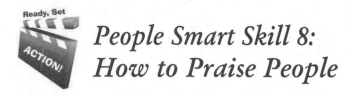

People Smart Skill 8:
How to Praise People

Attaining Excellence in this Area

Step 1   Analyze yourself on the techniques listed below.

Step 2   Check all the techniques you need to improve.

Step 3   Then for one week, or longer, practice these winning techniques until they are habits.

Concentrate on this one People Smart skill for this week only.

❑   I will be generous with praise.

❑   I will be sincere when I praise people.

❑   I will praise acts, not people.

❑   I will use the happiness formula, saying at least one kind thing to at least three people.

Turn the page to complete your
People Smart Journal for the next week.

Week in review

Use this section to create an action plan, celebrate successes and note important insights regarding this People Smart skill.

	Action/Goal	Results	Additional Thoughts
Sunday	------------------ ------------------ ------------------	------------------ ------------------ ------------------	------------------------------ ------------------------------ ------------------------------
Monday	------------------ ------------------ ------------------	------------------ ------------------ ------------------	------------------------------ ------------------------------ ------------------------------
Tuesday	------------------ ------------------ ------------------	------------------ ------------------ ------------------	------------------------------ ------------------------------ ------------------------------
Wednesday	------------------ ------------------ ------------------	------------------ ------------------ ------------------	------------------------------ ------------------------------ ------------------------------
Thursday	------------------ ------------------ ------------------	------------------ ------------------ ------------------	------------------------------ ------------------------------ ------------------------------
Friday	------------------ ------------------ ------------------	------------------ ------------------ ------------------	------------------------------ ------------------------------ ------------------------------
Saturday	------------------ ------------------ ------------------	------------------ ------------------ ------------------	------------------------------ ------------------------------ ------------------------------

How to Critique People

The sharpest of all tools is the human tongue so avoid the cutting edge when dealing with people. The key to successful criticism is the spirit in which it is given. The spirit in which the critique is given controls the results. If you wish to critique people to straighten them out or tell them off, you will reap mostly resentment. If you critique people for corrective purposes then this know-how will be most helpful.

Like everything else, there are good and poor critiques. Here are seven simple techniques for successful critiques of people:

1. *Nobody except the receiver should be listening, watching or knowing about the critique.* All criticism should be made in absolute privacy. It should be a dialogue between two people, not an example for many. This demonstrates that your criticism is constructive, not vindictive.

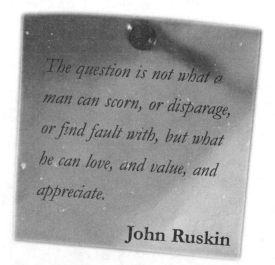

The question is not what a man can scorn, or disparage, or find fault with, but what he can love, and value, and appreciate.

John Ruskin

Never put people into the position of losing face, which is what happens when criticism is not made in private. However, when you want to make a criticism to a group as a warning or deterrent, focus on the action, not the person.

2. *Preface all criticism with a compliment or kind word.* Earlier we emphasized that the first few seconds of a relationship usually sets the tone and spirit of the entire relationship. Here is another example of that principle – preface all criticism with a positive. Create a friendly atmosphere. Make people more receptive before you voice your criticism.

Think about this like you would planting a garden. Before you plant your seed of critique, prepare the soil with kindness or a compliment. Here are a few examples:

Your work lately has been good; and we really need your attention on...

We appreciate the cooperation you have always given.
There is a point on which you could help...

Thank you for your help on that matter.
In the future, would you be careful not to...

3. *Make all criticism impersonal. Criticize the act, not the person.* When we talked about praise, we talked about praising the act, not the person. The same holds for criticism – criticize the act, not the person. If you focus on the act and not the person, you're more likely to get a favorable response. Remind yourself that you do not know most people well enough to criticize them personally, but you do have the right to criticize the action that you witness with your own eyes.

Wrong:	John, you are a problem.
Better:	John, we will not tolerate such poor work.

Wrong:	You are so dense!
Better:	This work shows that not much thought went into it.

4. *Supply the answer.* The answer means the right way; if you say something is wrong, then you should say what is right. Leadership is constructive criticism.

5. *Criticize just once.* The most justified criticism is said just once. Do not bring the matter up again, either directly or indirectly. If the criticism is disregarded, any future action will be on the disregard of the criticism, not the past action.

Criticism is like champagne; nothing more execrable if bad, nothing more excellent if good.

Charles Caleb Colton

6. *Don't demand.* First, ask for cooperation. It is human nature that you can get more cooperation from people by asking than demanding. Demanding is a last measure.

7. *Finish friendly.* Finish on a friendly note; let the last word be cordial. Reinforce the relationship, note that you consider the matter closed and that you'll continue to move forward, not look backward. Expect the same out of the person you critiqued. *This is the most important rule of the seven.*

Summary:

The key to a successful critique is the spirit in which it is given.

There are seven rules for successful critique:

1. All criticism should be in absolute privacy.

2. Preface all criticism with a kind word.

3. Make criticism impersonal. Criticize the act not the person.

4. Supply the answer and solutions.

5. Criticize just once.

6. Ask for cooperation.

7. Finish friendly.

Notes

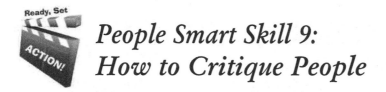

People Smart Skill 9:
How to Critique People

Attaining Excellence in this Area

Step 1   Analyze yourself on the techniques listed below.

Step 2   Check all the techniques you need to improve.

Step 3   Then for one week, or longer, practice these winning techniques until they are habits.

Concentrate on this one People Smart skill for this week only.

❑   I will voice my criticism in privacy.

❑   I will preface my criticism with compliments or kind words.

❑   I will criticize acts, not people.

❑   I will supply answers and solutions.

❑   I will criticize just once for each act.

❑   I will ask for, not demand, cooperation.

❑   I will finish friendly.

*Turn the page to complete your
People Smart Journal for the next week.*

Week in review

Use this section to create an action plan, celebrate successes and note important insights regarding this People Smart skill.

	Action/Goal	Results	Additional Thoughts
Sunday			
Monday			
Tuesday			
Wednesday			
Thursday			
Friday			
Saturday			

How to Thank People

It is the little things that make the big difference in skill with people. Gratitude and appreciation should be shown. Not only because it is nice or right, which it is, but because it is effective with people. It is not enough to think about how much you appreciate someone. Communicate it! One of the basic desires in people is to be appreciated. A weakness of many people is that they often don't show appreciation.

Learn the art of saying THANK YOU.

There is quite an art to saying thank you. All of us easily say the words thank you, but few of us know how to express our appreciation with grace, finesse and extreme effectiveness. This ability to say thank you effectively is so valuable because of human nature. The desire to be appreciated is one of the five basic drives in all of us. When we skillfully communicate our appreciation by saying thank you, we are both acting as civilized people and filling the other person's wants and needs.

All the beautiful sentiments in the world weigh less than a single lovely action.

James Russell Lowell

Being People Smart must, of necessity, include the art of saying **THANK YOU**. The ability to say Thank You effectively will really pay off.

Here are five simple rules for effectively saying thank you:

1. When you say thank you, mean it. Be sincere when you thank people. People know when you are sincere and when you are not sincere.

2. Say thank you clearly and distinctly. Say it as if you mean it; don't mumble, slur or whisper. Say it as if you are glad to be saying it.

3. Look at people when you thank them. It means so much more. Anybody worth thanking is worth looking at.

4. Thank people by name. Personalize all your thanks with names.

5. Work at thanking people. If any of us were to fall down, lose something or require assistance and someone were to help us, of course we would all have grace to say thank you. In countless normal situations – the obvious situations – the average person would quickly and sincerely say thank you, but this does not apply to the average situation. This applies to the not-so-obvious times when it requires thought, extra effort and time to say thank you.

Expressing your gratitude instead of taking for granted that the other person knows you appreciate their efforts and service – that is what is meant by working at thanking people. Make opportunities for thanking the supporting cast, the behind-the-scenes people (assistants, clerks, receptionists, mechanics), and everybody who needs to hear it. Write a note, make that phone call, or say it personally.

The extra effort and time taken to say thank you is exactly what separates the average person from the People Smart experts.

Summary:

Don't let people guess your feelings. Show your appreciation and gratitude. Learn the art of saying thank you.

1. When you say it, mean it

2. Say it clearly and distinctly.

3. Look at people when you thank them.

4. Thank them by name.

5. Work at thanking people: make that phone call, write that note, or say it in person.

Notes

_____

_____

_____

_____

_____

_____

_____

_____

_____

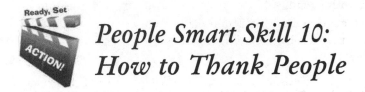

People Smart Skill 10:
How to Thank People

Attaining Excellence in this Area

Step 1   Analyze yourself on the techniques listed below.

Step 2   Check all the techniques you need to improve.

Step 3   Then for one week, or longer, practice these winning techniques until they are habits.

Concentrate on this one People Smart skill for this week only.

❑   I will be sincere when I say thank you.

❑   I will say thank you clearly and distinctly.

❑   I will look at people when I thank them.

❑   I will thank people by their names.

❑   I will work at thanking people for the little things as well as the obvious things.

Use the page on the right to complete your
People Smart Journal for the next week.

Week in review

Use this section to create an action plan, celebrate successes and note important insights regarding this People Smart skill.

	Action/Goal	Results	Additional Thoughts
Sunday			
Monday			
Tuesday			
Wednesday			
Thursday			
Friday			
Saturday			

Congratulations!

You have successfully completed this program. This is a fine accomplishment and you will reap the benefits for the rest of your life. Because you have had the strength and wisdom to have taken advantage of this excellent opportunity to help yourself and your family, a final suggestion......

A good number of people increase their benefits from this program by periodically repeating the 10 People Smart Skills. You will find it most worthwhile to do so, too.

Good Luck.

Les Giblin

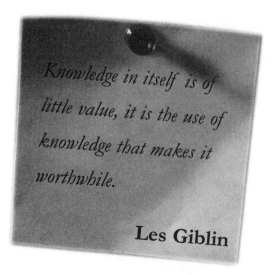

Knowledge in itself is of little value, it is the use of knowledge that makes it worthwhile.

Les Giblin

My Comments

_____
_____
_____
_____
_____
_____
_____
_____
_____
_____
_____
_____
_____
_____
_____
_____
_____
_____
_____
_____
_____
_____
_____
_____
_____
_____
_____
_____
_____

Notes

How to Be People Smart